Alberta D. Jones

BREAKOUT BEYOND
GAME GUIDE

*Advanced Strategies, Hidden Secrets, and
Pro Tips for Dominating Every Game Mode*

Chapter 1: Introduction to Breakout Beyond

1.1 The Legacy of Breakout: From Classic to Beyond

The Birth of a Gaming Icon

In 1976, Atari released **Breakout**, a simple yet addictive arcade game that became one of the defining titles of the early gaming era. Designed by **Nolan Bushnell, Steve Wozniak, and Steve Jobs**, the game featured a paddle-controlled ball that bounced off a wall of bricks, breaking them upon impact. The goal was to clear all the bricks while keeping the ball in play.

Breakout was a massive success, inspiring numerous clones and influencing the design of future arcade games. Its straightforward mechanics made it easy to learn but challenging to master, a formula that would persist for decades.

Breakout's Influence on the Gaming Industry

Breakout laid the foundation for many future games, both in terms of gameplay mechanics and technological innovation. It directly influenced titles such as **Arkanoid (1986)** by Taito, which expanded on the concept with power-ups and new brick types.

Beyond brick-breaking games, Breakout's simple yet engaging gameplay loop inspired developers to explore physics-based interactions in gaming. The mechanics of bouncing projectiles and precise paddle control can be seen in games like Pong, Peggle, and even certain pinball games.

Evolution Through the Years

As gaming hardware improved, so did the iterations of Breakout. The game saw multiple versions and adaptations across different platforms, including:

- **Super Breakout (1978)** – An enhanced version with additional game modes and improved graphics.
- **Breakout 2000 (1996)** – A 3D reimagining released on the Atari Jaguar, adding depth to the classic gameplay.
- **Breakout (2000, PlayStation 1)** – A fully reimagined version with adventure elements and a storyline.
- **Various Mobile & Browser Versions** – With the rise of mobile gaming, Breakout-inspired games became a staple on smartphones and web platforms.

Breakout Beyond: The Next Generation

Breakout Beyond builds upon the legacy of its predecessors while introducing a fresh perspective. Unlike the traditional **vertical** orientation of past games, Breakout Beyond adopts a **horizontal** gameplay approach, providing a new layer of strategy and movement dynamics.

With modern **graphics, power-ups, multiplayer modes, and procedural challenges**, Breakout Beyond aims to bring the classic formula to a new generation while retaining the fast-paced, skill-based gameplay that made the original a legend.

1.2 What's New in Breakout Beyond?

A Fresh Horizontal Perspective

Unlike previous versions of Breakout, which traditionally featured **vertical gameplay**, **Breakout Beyond** introduces a **horizontal playstyle**. This shift changes how players interact with the game, requiring new movement strategies and ball control techniques.

The horizontal layout allows for **wider level designs**, offering more room for creative challenges, different enemy placements, and **dynamic obstacles** that make gameplay feel fresh and modern.

New Power-Ups and Abilities

Breakout Beyond expands on the classic power-up system by introducing **new and improved abilities** that enhance gameplay. Some of the key power-ups include:

- **Multi-Ball:** Splits the ball into multiple balls for chaotic and high-scoring moments.
- **Laser Paddle:** Allows the paddle to fire lasers, breaking blocks directly.
- **Magnet Ball:** Enables the player to temporarily control the ball's movement.
- **Shield Booster:** Adds a protective barrier to prevent losing the ball easily.

These power-ups create **strategic depth**, allowing players to experiment with different combinations to maximize their efficiency.

Advanced Level Designs and Environmental Challenges

Breakout Beyond features **over 72 handcrafted levels**, each with **unique obstacles and mechanics**. Unlike classic Breakout games where levels consisted of static bricks, this version introduces:

- **Moving Blocks:** Bricks that shift positions, making timing crucial.
- **Hazards & Traps:** Spikes, fire zones, and energy fields that challenge precision.
- **Multi-Layered Levels:** Some stages require breaking through multiple layers before progressing.
- **Interactive Elements:** Switches, portals, and dynamic structures that alter gameplay.

These additions keep gameplay engaging and force players to **adapt their playstyle** to overcome new obstacles.

Multiplayer and Leaderboards

For the first time in a Breakout game, **Breakout Beyond** includes:

- **Local Co-Op Mode:** Play with a friend and work together to clear levels.
- **Online Leaderboards:** Compete against players worldwide for high scores.
- **Endless Mode:** A survival challenge where players compete for the longest run.

These features add **replay value and competitive play**, ensuring players always have new challenges to tackle.

Modern Graphics and Soundtrack

Breakout Beyond features **vibrant neon visuals**, futuristic animations, and **dynamic lighting effects** that make the game visually appealing. Additionally, the game's **synthwave-inspired soundtrack** creates an immersive and energetic experience, enhancing the thrill of breaking bricks.

1.3 Platforms and System Requirements

Available Platforms

Breakout Beyond is set to release across multiple platforms, ensuring accessibility for a wide range of players. The game will be available on:

- **PC (Steam & Epic Games Store)**
- **PlayStation 4 & PlayStation 5**
- **Xbox One & Xbox Series X/S**
- **Nintendo Switch**
- **Atari VCS**

Each version is optimized to take advantage of its respective platform, with **enhanced visuals, smooth gameplay performance, and controller support**.

Minimum and Recommended System Requirements (PC)

For PC gamers, ensuring that their system meets the requirements is crucial for a smooth experience. Below are the expected **minimum and recommended system requirements** for playing **Breakout Beyond** on a Windows PC.

Minimum Requirements:

- **OS:** Windows 10 (64-bit)
- **Processor:** Intel Core i3-7100 / AMD Ryzen 3 1200
- **Memory:** 4GB RAM
- **Graphics:** NVIDIA GeForce GTX 750 Ti / AMD Radeon R7 265
- **Storage:** 5GB available space
- **DirectX:** Version 11
- **Additional Notes:** Stable internet connection required for online features

Recommended Requirements:

- **OS:** Windows 11 (64-bit)
- **Processor:** Intel Core i5-9600K / AMD Ryzen 5 3600
- **Memory:** 8GB RAM
- **Graphics:** NVIDIA GeForce GTX 1060 / AMD Radeon RX 580
- **Storage:** 10GB available space
- **DirectX:** Version 12
- **Additional Notes:** SSD recommended for faster loading times

Performance on Consoles

- **PlayStation 5 & Xbox Series X/S:** 4K resolution at 60 FPS with enhanced visual effects
- **PlayStation 4 & Xbox One:** 1080p at 30-60 FPS, depending on performance mode
- **Nintendo Switch:** 720p (handheld) / 1080p (docked) at 30 FPS
- **Atari VCS:** Optimized to support smooth gameplay at 1080p

Cross-Platform Features

- **Cloud Saves (PC & Consoles):** Allows players to continue progress across different devices
- **Online Leaderboards:** Compete with global players across all platforms
- **Multiplayer Compatibility:** Local co-op available across all platforms

1.4 How to Use This Guide

Purpose of This Guide

This game guide for **Breakout Beyond** is designed to help players of all skill levels—whether you are a newcomer or a seasoned arcade veteran—understand the game's mechanics, strategies, and secrets. By following this guide, you will gain insights into **gameplay techniques, power-ups, level progression, and advanced strategies** to maximize your experience and performance in the game.

Guide Structure and Navigation

To make it easier for you to find the information you need, this guide is divided into **10 structured chapters**, each focusing on a key aspect of the game.

- **Chapter 1:** Introduction and Overview of Breakout Beyond
- **Chapter 2:** Getting Started (Installation, Controls, and Settings)
- **Chapter 3:** Core Gameplay Mechanics (Ball Physics, Paddle Movement, Scoring)

- **Chapter 4:** Game Modes and Challenges (Classic, Adventure, Endless, and Co-op)
- **Chapter 5:** Power-Ups and Special Abilities (How to Use Them Effectively)
- **Chapter 6:** Level Design and Environmental Hazards (Navigating Obstacles)
- **Chapter 7:** Advanced Strategies (Scoring, Leaderboards, Competitive Play)
- **Chapter 8:** Unlockables and Customization (Achievements, Skins, Easter Eggs)
- **Chapter 9:** Multiplayer and Online Features (Co-op, Leaderboards, DLCs)
- **Chapter 10:** Tips, Tricks, and Troubleshooting (FAQs, Performance Fixes)

Each chapter is **self-contained**, allowing you to jump directly to the section that interests you the most. However, for beginners, it is recommended to read through **Chapters 1–3** first to understand the game's fundamentals before diving into advanced strategies.

Key Features of This Guide

To help you quickly grasp important details, this guide includes:

- Detailed explanations of game mechanics, controls, and strategies
- Step-by-step instructions for different game modes and challenges
- Tips on maximizing power-ups and special abilities
- Advanced techniques for competitive play and leaderboard ranking
- Troubleshooting solutions for common technical issues

Who This Guide Is For

- **Beginners:** Learn the basics, understand game mechanics, and improve your skills.
- **Casual Players:** Get tips on power-ups, level progression, and fun game modes.
- **Competitive Players:** Discover high-score strategies, leaderboard tactics, and multiplayer tips.
- **Completionists:** Find all unlockables, Easter eggs, and hidden features.

How to Get the Most Out of This Guide

- **Read Sections as Needed:** No need to go through everything at once—jump to what you need.
- **Practice Alongside Reading:** Apply what you learn in real gameplay.
- **Experiment with Different Strategies:** Adapt tips and tricks to suit your playstyle.
- **Stay Updated:** Since the game may receive updates and new content, revisit the guide for new insights.

Chapter 2: Getting Started

2.1 Installing and Setting Up the Game

Downloading and Installing Breakout Beyond

Before jumping into the action, you need to install **Breakout Beyond** on your preferred platform. The game is available on **PC, PlayStation, Xbox, Nintendo Switch, and Atari VCS**. Follow the steps below for your specific system.

PC (Steam / Epic Games Store)

1. **Purchase the game** from Steam or the Epic Games Store.
2. **Download the game client** (Steam or Epic Games Launcher) if you haven't already.
3. **Log in** to your account.
4. **Search for "Breakout Beyond"** in the store and click the **Buy** or **Install** button.
5. Once the download is complete, **launch the game** from your library.

PlayStation (PS4 & PS5)

1. **Open the PlayStation Store** from the main menu.
2. **Search for "Breakout Beyond"** and select the game.
3. **Purchase and download** the game.
4. After installation, **navigate to your game library** and start playing.

Xbox (Xbox One & Xbox Series X/S)

1. **Go to the Microsoft Store** on your console.

2. **Search for "Breakout Beyond"** and purchase the game.
3. **Download and install** it to your console.
4. Once installed, **find the game in your library** and start playing.

Nintendo Switch

1. **Open the Nintendo eShop** from the home screen.
2. **Search for "Breakout Beyond"** and purchase the game.
3. **Download the game** and wait for the installation to finish.
4. The game will appear on your home screen, ready to launch.

Atari VCS

1. **Open the Atari VCS Store.**
2. **Locate and purchase** Breakout Beyond.
3. **Download and install** the game.
4. Start playing directly from the **VCS dashboard**.

Initial Setup and Settings

After installation, the first time you launch **Breakout Beyond**, you'll need to configure a few settings to optimize your gameplay experience.

Adjusting Display and Graphics

-   **PC:** Go to **Settings > Graphics** to adjust resolution, frame rate, and effects.
-   **Console:** The game auto-optimizes settings, but you can adjust brightness and motion blur in the settings menu.

Customizing Controls

- **Go to Settings > Controls** to check key bindings or button mappings.
- On **PC**, you can switch between **keyboard/mouse and controller**.
- On **consoles**, you can remap buttons for a comfortable setup.

Audio Settings

- Adjust **music, sound effects, and voiceover volume** to your preference.
- If using headphones, enable **3D Audio (PS5) or Spatial Sound (PC/Xbox)** for an immersive experience.

Creating or Linking Your Account

Some features, such as **online leaderboards and multiplayer**, require an account. Depending on your platform:

- **PC:** Sign in with Steam or Epic Games.
- **PlayStation/Xbox:** Your **PSN/Xbox Live** account is used automatically.
- **Nintendo Switch:** Uses your **Nintendo Account**.
- **Atari VCS:** Log in to your **Atari VCS profile**.

First-Time Playthrough

- Start with **Classic Mode** to get used to the mechanics.
- Experiment with **power-ups and ball control** before jumping into more challenging levels.
- Check out **the tutorial** if available to learn advanced moves.

2.2 Main Menu and Game Modes Overview

Navigating the Main Menu

When you launch **Breakout Beyond**, you will be taken to the **Main Menu**, which serves as the central hub for all game modes and settings. The menu is designed for quick navigation and easy access to different features. The main options available include:

- **Play** – Jump into different game modes.
- **Multiplayer** – Access co-op and online leaderboards.
- **Settings** – Customize controls, audio, and display settings.
- **Leaderboards** – Check global and personal rankings.
- **Customization** – Modify paddle skins, ball effects, and themes.
- **Achievements & Unlockables** – Track progress on milestones.

Each of these options provides access to different aspects of the game, ensuring a well-rounded experience.

Game Modes Overview

Breakout Beyond offers multiple game modes to suit different playstyles, from casual fun to competitive challenges. Below is a breakdown of each mode.

Classic Mode

- A modern take on the original **Breakout** experience.
- Players progress through **increasingly difficult levels** by breaking all bricks.

- Features **power-ups, obstacles, and dynamic physics** to keep gameplay engaging.
- Best suited for **new players and nostalgic fans** who want a traditional experience.

Adventure Mode

- A story-driven mode where players **explore different worlds** while breaking bricks.
- Includes **missions, boss battles, and environmental hazards**.
- Offers **power-up upgrades and character progression**.
- Great for players looking for an **immersive single-player experience**.

Endless Mode

- A **survival-based challenge** where players must keep the ball in play for as long as possible.
- Levels become progressively harder, introducing **new obstacles and speed increases**.
- Ideal for **players who enjoy high-score chasing and endurance challenges**.

Multiplayer Mode

- **Local Co-op**: Play with a friend in split-screen or shared-screen mode.
- **Online Leaderboards**: Compete for the highest scores against players worldwide.
- **Versus Mode**: Battle against another player by sending obstacles their way.
- Perfect for those who enjoy **competitive and cooperative gameplay**.

Challenge Mode

- A set of **pre-designed puzzles and objectives** that test skill and strategy.
- Includes time-based challenges, limited-move puzzles, and high-score objectives.
- Recommended for **players looking for a mix of strategy and reflex-based gameplay**.

Selecting Your Game Mode

To start a game mode:

1. Select **Play** from the Main Menu.
2. Choose from **Classic, Adventure, Endless, Multiplayer, or Challenge Mode**.
3. Adjust difficulty and game settings if available.
4. Press **Start** to begin playing.

2.3 Understanding the Controls and Settings

Basic Controls Overview

Mastering the controls is essential for precise gameplay in **Breakout Beyond**. Whether you're using a keyboard, controller, or touchscreen, responsive movement is key to success.

PC (Keyboard & Mouse Controls)

- **Move Paddle Left – A** or **Left Arrow**
- **Move Paddle Right – D** or **Right Arrow**
- **Launch Ball – Spacebar**

- Use Power-Up – **Enter** or **Left Click**
- **Pause/Menu – Esc**
- **Reset Level – R**

PC (Controller Support - Xbox/PlayStation)

- **Move Paddle Left – Left Stick (Left) / D-Pad Left**
- **Move Paddle Right – Left Stick (Right) / D-Pad Right**
- **Launch Ball – A (Xbox) / X (PlayStation)**
- **Use Power-Up – Right Trigger (RT/R2)**
- **Pause/Menu – Start (Xbox) / Options (PlayStation)**
- **Reset Level – Select / Touchpad**

Console Controls (PlayStation/Xbox/Nintendo Switch)

- **Move Paddle – Left Stick / D-Pad**
- **Launch Ball – Action Button (X/A/B, depending on console)**
- **Use Power-Up – Trigger Button (R2/ZR)**
- **Pause/Menu – Options/Menu Button**
- **Reset Level – Select Button**

Touchscreen Controls (Mobile/Nintendo Switch Handheld)

- **Swipe Left/Right** – Move Paddle
- **Tap Screen** – Launch Ball
- **Tap Power-Up Icon** – Activate Power-Up
- **Two-Finger Tap** – Pause Menu

Customizing Controls

Players can remap controls in the **Settings Menu** to match their preferences. To do this:

1. Navigate to **Settings > Controls** from the main menu.

2. Select **Key Bindings** or **Button Mapping** (depending on platform).
3. Choose the action you want to change and assign a new key/button.
4. Save changes and test them in practice mode.

Game Settings Overview

Breakout Beyond offers various **settings** to optimize gameplay based on your preferences and device capabilities.

Graphics Settings (PC & Next-Gen Consoles Only)

- **Resolution** – Adjust to match your screen size (720p, 1080p, 1440p, or 4K).
- **Frame Rate Limit** – Choose between **30 FPS, 60 FPS, or Unlimited FPS** (PC only).
- **Visual Effects** – Toggle motion blur, particle effects, and reflections.
- **Brightness & Contrast** – Adjust screen visibility for better gameplay clarity.

Audio Settings

- **Master Volume** – Controls all in-game audio.
- **Music Volume** – Adjusts background music level.
- **Sound Effects** – Modify ball bounce, explosion, and power-up sounds.
- **Voice Volume** – Adjusts any in-game voice prompts or narration.
- **Surround Sound** – Enables immersive audio on supported systems.

Gameplay Settings

- **Difficulty Level** – Choose from **Easy, Normal, Hard, or Extreme Mode**.
- **Ball Speed Modifier** – Adjust ball movement speed to fine-tune difficulty.
- **Paddle Sensitivity** – Change how fast the paddle moves based on input.
- **Power-Up Frequency** – Set how often power-ups appear during gameplay.
- **Vibration Feedback** – Enable/disable controller vibration effects.

Saving and Resetting Settings

If you need to restore settings to default:

1. Go to **Settings > Reset to Default**.
2. Confirm the reset, and all settings will return to their original values.

2.4 Customizing Your Gameplay Experience

Breakout Beyond offers a variety of customization options that allow players to personalize their experience, from visual aesthetics to gameplay mechanics. Whether you want to adjust the paddle's appearance, tweak difficulty settings, or enable accessibility options, this section will guide you through all the ways to tailor the game to your preferences.

Paddle and Ball Customization

Players can modify the look of their paddle and ball to suit their style.

Customizing the Paddle

- **Skins:** Unlock and apply different paddle designs. Some are earned through gameplay, while others are available as DLC.
- **Glow Effects:** Choose from different lighting and color effects for a unique visual experience.
- **Size Modifications:** In certain modes, you can adjust paddle size to increase or decrease difficulty.

Customizing the Ball

- **Ball Skins:** Change the ball's color, texture, or design. Some skins include special effects like a fire trail or neon glow.
- **Trail Effects:** Modify the particle effects that follow the ball's movement.
- **Ball Speed:** Adjust the initial speed of the ball for a faster or slower-paced game.

Difficulty and Game Modifiers

For players who want to fine-tune their gameplay challenge, **Breakout Beyond** offers a range of difficulty settings and game modifiers.

Difficulty Levels

- **Easy Mode:** Slower ball speed, wider paddle, and more frequent power-ups.
- **Normal Mode:** Standard game mechanics for a balanced experience.

- **Hard Mode:** Faster ball speed, smaller paddle, and fewer power-ups.
- **Extreme Mode:** Unpredictable ball physics, enemy obstacles, and additional challenges.

Custom Game Modifiers

Players can enable or disable specific gameplay mechanics:

- **Gravity Effects:** Alters ball physics, making it react differently to surfaces.
- **Power-Up Frequency:** Increase or decrease the rate at which power-ups appear.
- **Brick Durability:** Adjusts how many hits bricks require before breaking.
- **Score Multiplier:** Customize how points are awarded based on difficulty.

Accessibility Options

Breakout Beyond includes accessibility features to ensure an enjoyable experience for all players.

- **Colorblind Mode:** Adjusts colors to improve visibility for different types of color blindness.
- **High Contrast Mode:** Increases the visibility of game elements against the background.
- **Motion Reduction:** Disables excessive visual effects that may cause discomfort.
- **Adaptive Controls:** Allows remapping buttons and adjusting paddle movement sensitivity.
- **Assist Mode:** Slows down ball movement and increases paddle hit detection for players who need a less intense experience.

Audio and Visual Preferences

To enhance immersion or create a comfortable playing environment, players can adjust the game's sound and visual settings.

Sound Settings

- **Background Music:** Adjust volume or select different music tracks.
- **Sound Effects:** Modify bounce, explosion, and power-up sounds.
- **Voiceover:** Enable or disable in-game voice prompts.

Visual Settings

- **Screen Shake:** Enable or disable effects when hitting bricks or activating power-ups.
- **Bloom & Lighting Effects:** Toggle enhanced lighting for a more cinematic feel.
- **HUD Customization:** Adjust the placement or transparency of score displays and UI elements.

Saving and Applying Custom Settings

To ensure your customized settings are saved:

1. Navigate to **Settings > Customization** in the main menu.
2. Adjust options as desired.
3. Select **Apply Changes** to save your preferences.
4. If needed, use **Reset to Default** to return to the original game settings.

By customizing gameplay settings, visuals, and controls, you can create a **Breakout Beyond** experience that fits your playstyle, making each session more enjoyable and personalized.

Chapter 3: Core Gameplay Mechanics

3.1 How the Ball Physics Work

Understanding Ball Movement

In **Breakout Beyond**, the **ball physics** are crucial to gameplay, as they determine how the ball bounces, speeds up, and interacts with different surfaces. Unlike traditional arcade games, this version introduces **realistic physics with dynamic angles and momentum shifts**.

Key Ball Physics Mechanics:

- **Angle of Reflection:** The ball's bounce angle depends on where it hits the paddle or block.
- **Speed Scaling:** The ball gradually increases in speed after consecutive bounces, adding challenge.
- **Spin Mechanics:** Certain paddles allow players to apply spin, affecting the ball's trajectory.
- **Friction & Gravity Effects:** Some game modes introduce variable gravity and air resistance.

How Bounce Angles Work

- **Center of the Paddle:** A straight bounce with minimal angle deviation.
- **Edges of the Paddle:** Causes sharper angles, useful for strategic aiming.
- **Corner Hits:** Adds unpredictability to the ball's direction.

Momentum and Acceleration

- Hitting power-ups or **special surfaces** can alter ball speed.
- Some power-ups, like **Slow Motion**, temporarily reduce speed.
- If the ball moves too fast, players must react quickly to avoid losing control.

Mastering these physics helps players **strategically aim** and **control gameplay pace**.

3.2 Paddle Movement and Control Techniques

Basic Paddle Movements

The paddle is the primary tool for directing the ball, and its movement mechanics are key to success.

- **Standard Movement:** Move left or right using keys, a controller stick, or touch gestures.
- **Precision Control:** Some settings allow fine-tuned movement for better accuracy.
- **Momentum Carry:** Sudden directional shifts can impact how the ball rebounds.

Advanced Paddle Techniques

- **Soft Deflections:** Slightly tapping the ball instead of forceful rebounds helps with precise aiming.
- **Power Shots:** Quick paddle movements at impact can increase ball speed.

- **Spin Control:** In some modes, paddles can apply spin for curved shots.
- **Edge Bounces:** Using paddle edges to redirect the ball into tricky angles.

Mastering these techniques will improve overall gameplay efficiency.

3.3 Breaking Blocks: Scoring and Strategies

How Scoring Works

Players earn points based on the **type of block destroyed, combos, and power-ups used**.

- **Basic Blocks:** Standard points per hit.
- **Multi-Hit Blocks:** Extra points for breaking them completely.
- **Chain Reactions:** Consecutive hits without letting the ball drop increase combo multipliers.
- **Power-Up Blocks:** Provide **bonus points** and temporary effects.

Strategies for Efficient Scoring

- **Corner Traps:** Getting the ball stuck in a loop near blocks maximizes destruction.
- **Angle Manipulation:** Using the paddle to aim at weak points in block formations.
- **Combo Chains:** Keeping the ball in motion without a miss increases score multipliers.

- **Targeting Power-Ups:** Breaking specific blocks first can unlock powerful abilities.

A balance of **precision, speed, and timing** will help maximize scores.

3.4 Managing Lives and Game Over Conditions

Understanding the Life System

- Players start with **a set number of lives** (varies by difficulty).
- A life is lost if the ball **falls below the paddle** without a safety net (if available).
- Some power-ups or achievements grant **extra lives**.

Game Over Conditions

- **Single-Player:** The game ends when all lives are lost.
- **Endless Mode:** Players continue until they fail to sustain ball movement.
- **Multiplayer Mode:** Lives may be shared or individual, depending on game settings.

Preventing Game Over

- Use **paddle positioning** effectively to avoid missing the ball.
- Activate **extra life power-ups** when possible.
- Learn and master **ball control techniques** for better survival chances.

With practice, players can **extend gameplay time, maintain high scores, and survive longer in harder levels**.

Chapter 4: Game Modes Explained

4.1 Classic Mode: Traditional Breakout Experience

Overview of Classic Mode

Classic Mode is a **modernized take on the traditional Breakout formula**, where players aim to clear all blocks in a level using a bouncing ball and a movable paddle. This mode stays true to the core mechanics that made the original game a hit while integrating enhanced visuals, power-ups, and physics for a refined experience.

How Classic Mode Works

- Players start with **a set number of lives**.
- The objective is to **break all blocks** on the screen before running out of lives.
- The ball **increases in speed** over time, making it progressively harder to control.
- Players can collect **power-ups** to gain temporary advantages.

Difficulty Settings in Classic Mode

- **Easy Mode:** Slower ball speed, larger paddle, and frequent power-ups.
- **Normal Mode:** Standard gameplay mechanics.

- **Hard Mode:** Faster ball speed, smaller paddle, and fewer power-ups.
- **Extreme Mode:** Unpredictable ball physics and additional obstacles.

Best Strategies for Classic Mode

- **Corner Looping:** Aim for corners to get the ball trapped in a loop for continuous block destruction.
- **Controlled Paddle Movement:** Move smoothly to avoid unpredictable bounces.
- **Prioritize Power-Ups:** Some power-ups (like the Multi-Ball) can clear levels faster.
- **Watch for Speed Increases:** Prepare for faster ball movement as levels progress.

4.2 Adventure Mode: Level Progression and Challenges

What Makes Adventure Mode Unique?

Unlike Classic Mode, Adventure Mode **introduces structured level progression, unique challenges, and narrative elements**. Each stage comes with different layouts, obstacles, and mission-based objectives that add variety to gameplay.

Features of Adventure Mode

- **Progressive Level System:** Each stage is uniquely designed with increasing difficulty.
- **Missions & Objectives:** Players may need to **unlock specific power-ups, defeat bosses, or clear levels within a time limit**.

- **Themed Environments:** Levels take place in distinct worlds, each with its own aesthetics and challenges.
- **Unlockable Rewards:** Completing stages unlocks **new paddle skins, ball effects, and secret levels.**

Challenges in Adventure Mode

- **Boss Battles:** Certain levels feature AI-controlled bosses that require strategic play.
- **Environmental Hazards:** Moving obstacles, gravity shifts, and wind effects can change ball trajectory.
- **Limited Power-Ups:** Some levels restrict power-ups, requiring precise skill to progress.

Tips for Adventure Mode

- **Adapt to Level Design:** Study the layout before making your first shot.
- **Utilize Power-Ups Wisely:** Save key power-ups for tougher sections of a level.
- **Anticipate Boss Patterns:** Learn attack cycles and weak points in boss battles.

4.3 Endless Mode: Surviving the Longest

What is Endless Mode?

Endless Mode is a **survival-based challenge** where players must keep the ball in play for as long as possible. Unlike other modes, the objective is not to clear all blocks but to **score as high as possible before losing all lives.**

Key Mechanics of Endless Mode

- **Increasing Difficulty:** The ball gets **faster over time**, and new obstacles appear.
- **Randomized Block Layouts:** No two runs are the same, as the block arrangement changes each round.
- **Limited Power-Ups:** Some power-ups appear less frequently, making survival harder.
- **Combo Multiplier System:** Consecutive hits without losing the ball build up score multipliers.

Survival Tips for Endless Mode

- **Stay Near the Center:** This gives better reaction time for unexpected ball movements.
- **Prioritize Extra Lives:** Collect life-boosting power-ups whenever possible.
- **Maintain Combo Chains:** Keeping a high multiplier will help maximize your score.
- **Use Angled Shots:** Keeping the ball moving unpredictably can help it stay in play longer.

4.4 Local Co-op: Playing with Friends

How Local Co-op Works

Local Co-op Mode allows **two players to team up** and play together on the same screen. This mode is designed for fun, collaborative gameplay and requires teamwork to succeed.

Types of Local Co-op Modes

- **Shared Paddle Mode:** Both players control the same paddle, requiring coordination.
- **Split Paddle Mode:** Each player controls their own paddle, positioned on opposite sides.
- **Versus Mode:** Players compete to see who can score the most points before a time limit.

Best Strategies for Co-op Mode

- **Communicate with Your Partner:** Decide who covers which area of the screen.
- **Take Advantage of Two Paddles:** In Split Paddle Mode, use teamwork to trap the ball in corners.
- **Coordinate Power-Up Usage:** Some power-ups affect both players, so plan when to activate them.

Why Play Local Co-op?

- **More Fun with Friends:** Perfect for couch gaming sessions.
- **Competitive Edge:** Challenge each other for the highest score.
- **Team-Based Strategy:** Working together makes high-level play more engaging.

With these modes explained, players can choose the game style that best suits their preference, whether it's **classic arcade action, an immersive adventure, endless survival, or co-op fun**!

Chapter 5: Power-Ups and Special Abilities

5.1 Types of Power-Ups and Their Effects

Power-ups in **Breakout Beyond** add an extra layer of strategy and excitement, allowing players to manipulate the ball, paddle, and even the playing field. These power-ups can be collected by hitting special blocks or completing certain in-game objectives.

Offensive Power-Ups

- **Multi-Ball:** Splits the ball into multiple copies, increasing destruction speed.
- **Fireball:** The ball passes through multiple bricks without bouncing.
- **Explosive Ball:** Causes a small explosion on impact, breaking nearby bricks.
- **Laser Paddle:** Equips the paddle with a laser cannon to shoot and destroy bricks.

Defensive Power-Ups

- **Extended Paddle:** Temporarily increases paddle width for better control.
- **Sticky Paddle:** The ball sticks to the paddle for precise aiming before release.
- **Shield Barrier:** A protective shield appears below the paddle, saving the ball from being lost once.
- **Slow Motion:** Temporarily slows the ball's speed for better reaction time.

Utility Power-Ups

- **Magnet Ball:** The ball is drawn toward certain blocks, making aiming easier.
- **Time Stop:** Freezes all blocks in place, preventing movement-based obstacles.
- **Point Multiplier:** Doubles or triples the score earned for a limited time.
- **Gravity Shift:** Changes ball physics, allowing unique bounce angles.

Negative Power-Ups (Debuffs)

- **Shrink Paddle:** Reduces paddle size, making it harder to hit the ball.
- **Speed Boost:** Dramatically increases the ball's velocity, making it difficult to control.
- **Reverse Controls:** Temporarily inverts paddle movement.
- **Blackout:** Darkens the screen, reducing visibility for a few seconds.

5.2 When and How to Use Power-Ups

Using power-ups strategically can mean the difference between victory and defeat. Some power-ups work best when activated at the right moment.

Best Situations for Offensive Power-Ups

- **Multi-Ball:** Use when there are many blocks left, but avoid if you struggle to track multiple balls.
- **Fireball & Explosive Ball:** Activate when facing multi-hit or reinforced blocks.

- **Laser Paddle:** Use when bricks are difficult to reach with normal ball movement.

When to Use Defensive Power-Ups

- **Extended Paddle:** Activate if the ball is moving too fast for comfort.
- **Sticky Paddle:** Use for precision aiming when targeting a difficult spot.
- **Shield Barrier:** Keep as a backup in challenging levels.

Utility Power-Ups and Their Best Use Cases

- **Point Multiplier:** Activate when you have a **high combo streak** to maximize score.
- **Gravity Shift:** Use in levels with tricky layouts to create new angles of attack.
- **Magnet Ball:** Activate when precision is necessary, such as in puzzle-style levels.

5.3 Managing Multiple Power-Ups Strategically

Players can collect multiple power-ups at once, but choosing the right combinations can be key to success.

Stacking Compatible Power-Ups

Some power-ups work well together:

- **Multi-Ball + Point Multiplier:** Maximize score gain with multiple active balls.

- **Sticky Paddle + Fireball:** Helps aim fireballs precisely for maximum block destruction.
- **Extended Paddle + Shield Barrier:** Offers maximum defense during high-speed gameplay.

Avoiding Harmful Combinations

Not all power-ups should be used together:

- **Multi-Ball + Speed Boost:** Makes it too hard to track all balls.
- **Slow Motion + Explosive Ball:** Slows the game down when an explosive approach would be better.
- **Gravity Shift + Magnet Ball:** Can cause unpredictable ball behavior.

Power-Up Prioritization

If multiple power-ups appear at once:

1. **Choose defensive power-ups first** if struggling to keep the ball in play.
2. **Go for offensive power-ups** if clearing blocks is the priority.
3. **Use utility power-ups last** to gain extra advantages after the play area is secure.

5.4 Unlocking Hidden Special Abilities

Beyond standard power-ups, **Breakout Beyond** features hidden special abilities that can be unlocked through challenges and achievements.

How to Unlock Special Abilities

- **High Score Mastery:** Reach specific point thresholds in different modes.
- **Secret Level Completions:** Some levels hide special ability unlocks.
- **Perfect Streaks:** Consecutive level wins without losing a life may reward unique abilities.
- **Power-Up Mastery:** Using certain power-ups a set number of times unlocks enhanced versions.

Examples of Special Abilities

- **Infinity Ball:** A ball that never slows down and can only be lost after a set time.
- **Warp Shot:** Allows the ball to teleport to a selected location on the board.
- **Supercharged Laser Paddle:** Fires stronger lasers that destroy multiple bricks at once.
- **Time Rewind:** Briefly reverses time, restoring the last few seconds of gameplay.

Using Special Abilities Wisely

- Special abilities often have **limited uses** per game session.
- Save them for **boss battles or extremely difficult levels**.
- Some abilities have cooldown timers, so plan ahead before activating them.

By mastering power-ups and unlocking **hidden abilities**, players can greatly enhance their **Breakout Beyond** experience, making gameplay more dynamic, strategic, and rewarding.

Chapter 6: Level Design and Challenges

6.1 Understanding Different Level Layouts

Breakout Beyond introduces a **variety of level designs** that challenge players with unique block arrangements, obstacles, and gameplay twists. Understanding these layouts is crucial for strategic play and efficient progression.

Common Level Layout Types

1. **Classic Grid Layout**

   - Standard rectangular block arrangements.
   - Best approached with **angled shots** to maximize block-breaking efficiency.

2. **Maze-Like Structures**

   - Blocks form **intricate patterns**, requiring precise ball control.
   - Players may need to **bounce the ball off walls** to reach hidden areas.

3. **Stacked Layers**

   - Blocks are positioned in overlapping layers, with **multi-hit blocks on top**.
   - The challenge is to **break through outer layers before reaching inner blocks**.

4. **Moving Block Patterns**

   - Some levels have **dynamic elements**, with blocks shifting positions over time.
   - Timing is key to hitting blocks before they move away.

5. **Gravity-Affected Levels**

   - Certain stages introduce **low gravity or directional gravity shifts**.
   - Players must adapt their paddle movements to compensate for ball trajectory changes.

Strategies for Different Layouts

- **Use Power-Ups Wisely**: In **stacked levels**, fireballs or explosive balls clear multiple layers faster.
- **Angle the Ball for Maximum Impact**: In **maze-like designs**, bounce the ball at sharp angles to reach inaccessible spots.
- **Observe Movement Patterns**: In **dynamic layouts**, wait for the right moment before taking a shot.

6.2 Environmental Hazards and How to Avoid Them

Many levels in **Breakout Beyond** introduce environmental hazards that add extra difficulty. These elements **affect ball movement, paddle control, or level progression**, requiring players to adapt their strategies.

Types of Environmental Hazards

1. Moving Obstacles

- Some levels include barriers that shift, **blocking the ball's path temporarily.**
- **Avoidance Tip: Time your shots** so the ball bounces off when the barrier moves away.

2. Unbreakable Blocks

- Indestructible barriers force players to **find alternate ball angles.**
- **Avoidance Tip:** Aim for gaps between unbreakable blocks to **target breakable areas.**

3. Speed Zones

- Some areas of the screen **increase the ball's speed** drastically upon contact.
- **Avoidance Tip:** Keep the paddle **centered** to react quickly when the ball returns.

4. Reverse Control Zones

- Certain areas **temporarily invert paddle movement,** making control harder.
- **Avoidance Tip:** Move cautiously in these zones and prepare to adjust control habits.

5. Teleportation Portals

- The ball enters one portal and exits from another, **changing its trajectory unpredictably.**

- **Avoidance Tip:** Learn portal exit points early and adjust your paddle position accordingly.

General Strategies for Avoiding Hazards

- **Memorize hazard positions** before making risky shots.
- **Use slow-motion power-ups** if available, to navigate tricky sections.
- **Adjust your timing** based on obstacle movement patterns.

6.3 Puzzle Elements and Hidden Paths

Some levels in **Breakout Beyond** feature **puzzle-like mechanics**, where simply breaking blocks isn't enough to progress. Instead, players must figure out the best way to unlock hidden areas, trigger special effects, or manipulate the environment to succeed.

Types of Puzzle Elements

1. Switch-Activated Blocks

- Certain blocks are **locked until a switch is activated** by hitting a specific target.
- **Solution:** Identify switch blocks early and aim the ball to trigger them as soon as possible.

2. Color-Coded Block Chains

- Some blocks are linked by color, meaning **breaking one can clear all matching blocks**.
- **Solution:** Prioritize breaking key blocks to create cascading effects.

3. Time-Limited Doors

- Some levels have **doors or walls that open and close** at intervals.
- **Solution:** Observe door timing and aim carefully to send the ball through when open.

4. Multi-Hit Hidden Paths

- Some breakable walls require **multiple hits** before revealing secret paths.
- **Solution:** Focus on **areas that look suspicious**—hidden paths often lead to **bonus rewards or shortcuts**.

How to Find Hidden Paths

- **Aim for corner areas:** Hidden paths are often tucked behind walls or tough-to-reach spots.
- **Look for slight color differences:** Some breakable walls look slightly different than normal ones.
- **Use power-ups to your advantage:** Explosive or fireball power-ups help reveal secret areas faster.

By learning how to manipulate these puzzle elements, players can **unlock secret areas, earn bonus points, and access exclusive rewards**.

6.4 Adapting to Increasing Difficulty

As players progress in **Breakout Beyond**, levels become **more complex, faster-paced, and filled with obstacles**. Adapting to these changes is key to mastering the game.

How Difficulty Increases

- **Faster Ball Speed:** As levels progress, the ball moves **faster**, requiring quicker reflexes.
- **Tougher Block Patterns:** Levels feature **more unbreakable blocks, moving platforms, and tricky angles**.
- **More Hazards:** Reverse controls, teleporters, and speed boosts become more common.
- **Limited Power-Ups:** The game provides **fewer helpful power-ups**, forcing reliance on skill.

Tips for Adapting to Harder Levels

1. Improve Reaction Time

- **Stay centered** with the paddle to react faster.
- Use **slower ball angles** to give yourself more time to prepare for the next hit.

2. Master Ball Control

- Learn how to **use paddle angles** to control ball movement.
- Use the **Sticky Paddle power-up** for precise aiming.

3. Prioritize Key Blocks

- Target **multi-hit blocks or switches** early to open up easier paths.
- If levels have **limited space**, focus on clearing the center first.

4. Conserve Power-Ups for Later Stages

- Don't waste strong power-ups on **early, easy sections** of a level.
- Save shields, fireballs, and laser paddles for when **block density increases**.

Chapter 7: Advanced Strategies for High Scores

7.1 Perfecting Your Reflexes and Timing

In **Breakout Beyond**, success often depends on **quick reflexes and precise timing**. As the ball speed increases and obstacles become more challenging, mastering these skills is essential for high-score runs.

How to Improve Reflexes

- **Stay focused on the ball**: Avoid distractions and train your eyes to follow the ball's movement at all times.
- **Use peripheral vision**: Instead of fixating on the paddle, develop the ability to track both the ball and upcoming obstacles simultaneously.
- **Practice with high-speed levels**: Playing in **Endless Mode** or against fast-paced levels can help sharpen reflexes.

Timing Your Paddle Movements

- **Wait for the right moment**: Swinging too early or late can send the ball in unpredictable directions.
- **Learn to adjust on the fly**: React to last-second changes, such as the ball hitting an unexpected angle or a moving block.
- **Use slow-motion power-ups wisely**: If available, activating **slow-motion** during high-speed sequences can help regain control.

Drills to Enhance Reflexes

- **Warm up in slower game modes** before tackling harder levels.
- **Deliberately play at increased speeds** to force quick reactions.
- **Challenge yourself with unpredictable shots** by making angled plays and deflections.

With **consistent practice and focus**, players can significantly improve reaction times, making even the hardest levels **more manageable**.

7.2 Angle Control and Predicting Ball Movement

Mastering **angle control** is one of the most important skills for reaching high scores in **Breakout Beyond**. Since the ball's trajectory depends on where it strikes the paddle, precise control allows players to **aim for optimal rebounds** and maintain long streaks.

Understanding Ball Angles

- **Center Hits → Straight Shots**: If the ball hits the center of the paddle, it will bounce **directly upward**.
- **Edge Hits → Sharper Angles**: Striking near the paddle's edges causes the ball to **bounce at extreme angles**, useful for reaching corners.
- **Slightly Off-Center Hits → Controlled Angles**: Adjusting the ball's trajectory slightly allows for **fine control over shot placement**.

Strategies for Predicting Ball Movement

- **Observe the bounce pattern**: Blocks and walls reflect the ball at equal angles—use this to plan ahead.
- **Pre-position the paddle**: Move into the expected landing zone **before the ball reaches your area**.
- **Use walls to your advantage**: Banking the ball off walls can help clear out **hard-to-reach blocks**.

Angle Tricks for High Scores

- **Zig-Zag Shot**: Hit the ball at alternating angles to maximize the number of block hits per bounce.
- **Wall Bounce Trick**: If a direct shot isn't possible, bouncing off a sidewall can create unexpected attack paths.
- **Delayed Drop Shot**: If power-ups like **Sticky Paddle** are available, use them to **pause and aim for precision shots**.

7.3 Maximizing Score Multipliers and Combos

Achieving **high scores** in *Breakout Beyond* isn't just about surviving—it's about **chaining combos and maximizing multipliers** to rack up points efficiently. By keeping the ball in play and utilizing strategic shot placement, players can drastically increase their scores.

How Score Multipliers Work

- **Consecutive Hits Increase Multipliers**: Each time the ball breaks a block without missing, the multiplier **gradually increases**.

- **Losing the Ball Resets the Multiplier**: If the ball is lost, the multiplier **drops to its default level**.
- **Special Blocks Provide Bonus Multipliers**: Some bricks have **score-boosting effects** when broken.

Best Strategies for Maximizing Multipliers

1. **Keep the Ball in Motion**

   - Avoid missing shots by positioning the paddle **early**.
   - Use the **Sticky Paddle** power-up to line up precision shots that maintain streaks.

2. **Focus on Chain Reactions**

   - Use **Multi-Ball** power-ups to **keep multiple balls bouncing**, increasing combo potential.
   - Break **color-linked blocks** in succession for extra point boosts.

3. **Target Special Blocks First**

   - Some bricks grant **double or triple multipliers—** prioritize breaking them.
   - Use **angle control** to aim for these blocks before regular ones.

4. **Use Power-Ups to Extend Combos**

   - Fireball and explosive effects **hit multiple blocks at once**, boosting score gains.
   - Slow-motion power-ups help maintain streaks when ball speed increases.

5. **Avoid Panic Movements**

   - Rushing shots often leads to mistakes and missed combos.

- Focus on **controlled, well-placed bounces** to extend the multiplier.

7.4 Competing in Online Leaderboards

For players who want to **prove their skills**, *Breakout Beyond* features **online leaderboards** where they can compete against others for the highest scores.

How Online Leaderboards Work

- **Global & Regional Rankings**: Compare scores with players worldwide or within specific regions.
- **Weekly & Monthly Tournaments**: Compete in limited-time events for exclusive rewards.
- **Friends & Private Leaderboards**: Challenge friends and track progress in private leaderboards.

Best Practices for Climbing the Leaderboards

1. **Optimize High-Score Runs**

   - Play in **Endless Mode or Challenge Mode**, where higher scores are more achievable.
   - **Memorize level patterns** to improve efficiency in scoring.

2. **Use Score-Boosting Power-Ups Efficiently**

   - Save **point multipliers** for **long combo streaks**.
   - Activate **Multi-Ball** only when it will be manageable—losing balls can break combos.

3. **Perfect Your Timing & Angles**

- o **Master ball control** to keep shots consistent.
- o Avoid unnecessary risks that might reset the multiplier.

4. **Learn from Top Players**

   - o Watch **replays or strategy videos** from top leaderboard players.
   - o Study their **paddle positioning, shot angles, and power-up usage**.

5. **Compete in Events for Bonus Rewards**

   - o Some limited-time leaderboard events **offer double multipliers** or unique power-ups.
   - o Participating in special modes **increases your ranking potential**.

Chapter 8: Unlockables and Customization

8.1 Unlockable Skins and Paddle Designs

Breakout Beyond offers a variety of **skins and paddle designs** that allow players to personalize their gameplay experience. These cosmetic options don't affect performance but provide a **unique visual style** and can be unlocked through progression, achievements, or in-game challenges.

Types of Unlockable Skins

- **Classic Skins**: Retro-style designs inspired by the original *Breakout*.
- **Futuristic Skins**: Neon-lit paddles and balls with sci-fi aesthetics.
- **Elemental Skins**: Fire, ice, and lightning-themed visuals that add cool effects.
- **Themed Event Skins**: Limited-time designs available during special game events.

Ways to Unlock Skins and Paddle Designs

1. **Progression Unlocks**

   - Certain paddle designs become available by **reaching new level milestones**.
   - Players unlock new skins by **completing adventure mode challenges**.

2. **Achievement-Based Rewards**

   - Breaking a specific number of blocks or achieving high scores grants exclusive skins.
   - Finishing a level without losing a ball may reward a **rare paddle skin**.

3. **Leaderboard and Event Rewards**

   - Top-ranked players in **weekly or monthly leaderboards** earn **unique skins**.
   - Seasonal events introduce **limited-edition customization options**.

4. **In-Game Store or Microtransactions**

   - Some skins can be **purchased with in-game currency or real money**.
   - Special bundles offer **theme packs with matching paddles and ball designs**.

Customizing Your Paddle

- Players can access their unlocked designs via the **Customization Menu**.
- Certain skins include **animated effects** or **trails that follow the ball**.
- Customization options help players **stand out in multiplayer and leaderboard rankings**.

Unlocking and using different skins **adds a personal touch** to *Breakout Beyond*, making every game feel unique!

8.2 Earning Achievements and Rewards

Achievements in *Breakout Beyond* provide **long-term goals** and reward players with **bonus content** like skins, in-game currency, and leaderboard points.

Types of Achievements

1. Progression Achievements

- Earned by **completing levels and advancing through Adventure Mode**.
- Examples:
    - *First Break* – Break your first block.
    - *Beyond Beginner* – Complete the first 10 levels.

2. Skill-Based Achievements

- Awarded for performing advanced gameplay techniques.
- Examples:
    - *Sharpshooter* – Hit 10 blocks in a row without missing.
    - *Perfect Run* – Complete a level without losing a ball.

3. Combo and Scoring Achievements

- Achievements tied to **multipliers, streaks, and high scores**.
- Examples:
    - *Combo Master* – Maintain a 10x multiplier.
    - *Millionaire* – Score over 1,000,000 points in a single game.

4. Secret & Easter Egg Achievements

- Hidden challenges that require **discovering secrets in the game**.
- Examples:
    - *Hidden Path* – Find a secret level entrance.
    - *Retro Revival* – Unlock a classic *Breakout* mode.

How to Claim Rewards

- **Achievements grant rewards** such as:
    - **New paddle and ball designs.**
    - **Bonus power-ups for gameplay.**
    - **Leaderboard ranking boosts.**
- Players can **track their progress** in the **Achievements Menu**.
- Some **rare achievements unlock trophies or badges** for online profiles.

8.3 Secret Levels and Easter Eggs

Breakout Beyond hides **secret levels and Easter eggs** throughout the game, rewarding curious players with **bonus challenges, nostalgic throwbacks, and exclusive unlockables**.

How to Unlock Secret Levels

1. **Breaking Hidden Blocks**

    - Some levels contain **invisible or reinforced blocks** that, when broken, reveal a portal to a **hidden stage**.

- Look for **blocks that don't react normally** to ball hits—they may need multiple strikes or a power-up to reveal the entrance.

2. **Entering Special Code Sequences**

   - In some game modes, entering a **specific sequence of movements or button inputs** at the main menu can unlock hidden content.
   - Example: Entering the **original Atari Breakout paddle sequence** might unlock a **retro-themed level**.

3. **Achieving High Scores in a Single Run**

   - Some secret levels are unlocked by **scoring above a certain threshold** without losing a life.
   - Players who maintain **long combo streaks** are more likely to access these levels.

4. **Interacting with Background Elements**

   - Some levels have **interactive scenery**—hitting certain objects or walls multiple times might trigger a **secret warp zone**.

Easter Eggs Hidden in the Game

- **Retro Breakout Mode**: A hidden setting that reverts graphics and sound effects to the **original 1976 Breakout style**.
- **Developer Signatures**: Some levels contain **initials or hidden messages** from the game's developers.
- **Classic Game References**: Look for nods to **other arcade classics**, such as Pong or Space Invaders, hidden in background art or level names.

- **Mystery Power-Ups**: Rare power-ups with **unexpected effects**, like reversing time or slowing down the ball for extended combos.

By exploring and experimenting with different in-game mechanics, players can **discover hidden surprises and unique challenges** in *Breakout Beyond*!

8.4 Customizing Visual and Audio Settings

Customization extends beyond paddle skins and game modes— *Breakout Beyond* allows players to **tweak visual and audio settings** to enhance their experience.

Visual Customization Options

1. **Graphics Modes**

   - **Classic Pixel Mode**: Gives the game a retro, arcade-style look.
   - **HD Modern Mode**: Smooth animations, high-quality textures, and particle effects.

2. **Background Themes**

   - Choose from a variety of backgrounds, including:
     - **Space Nebula** (glowing stars and planets)
     - **Cyber Grid** (neon lights and digital effects)
     - **Minimalist Mode** (distraction-free, simple colors)

3. **Ball & Paddle Effects**

   - Enable **trails, glow effects, or unique ball colors**.

- Adjust **ball size or speed effects** for a different visual feel.

4. **Accessibility Options**

   - **Colorblind Mode**: Adjusts block colors for better visibility.
   - **Reduced Motion Mode**: Disables excessive visual effects for smoother gameplay.

Audio Customization Options

1. **Music & Sound Effects**

   - Toggle background music between:
     - **Classic Arcade Tunes**
     - **Synthwave Beats**
     - **Relaxing Ambient Tracks**
   - Adjust sound effect levels for **ball bounces, block breaks, and power-up activations**.

2. **Announcer & Voice Settings**

   - Enable or disable **voice commentary** for a more arcade-like feel.
   - Change announcer styles from **retro robotic** to **modern energetic voices**.

3. **Dynamic Audio Mode**

   - Music changes dynamically based on in-game action (e.g., **faster-paced beats when ball speed increases**).

By adjusting these settings, players can create a **personalized, immersive gaming experience** that suits their style and preferences in *Breakout Beyond*!

Chapter 9: Multiplayer and Online Features

9.1 Local Co-op: Working Together for Success

Breakout Beyond offers a **local co-op mode**, allowing two players to **team up on the same screen** to break blocks together. This mode introduces unique **cooperative mechanics and challenges** that require teamwork and communication.

How Local Co-op Works

- **Shared Paddle Control**: In some modes, both players control a **single, larger paddle**, requiring synchronized movement.
- **Dual-Paddle Mode**: Each player controls their **own paddle**, positioned on opposite sides of the screen.
- **Split Lives System**: Players share a **limited number of lives**, so strategic coordination is key.

Co-op Strategies for Success

1. **Coordinate Paddle Movements**

   - Avoid moving **in the same direction** at the wrong time, which can leave gaps.
   - Communicate when switching positions to **cover more space effectively**.

2. **Divide Responsibilities**

    o One player can focus on **deflecting the ball**, while the other prioritizes **hitting power-ups**.
    o If playing with **two paddles**, assign roles such as **offense (aiming at blocks) and defense (saving the ball from falling)**.
3. **Utilize Power-Ups Wisely**

    o Some power-ups affect both players—decide in advance **who will collect which ones**.
    o If one player has a stronger angle control, let them grab **multi-ball or fireball abilities**.
4. **Keep the Ball in Play**

    o The longer the ball stays in motion, the higher the **score multiplier grows**.
    o If both players are actively rebounding shots, combos build faster.

Playing in **local co-op mode** provides a **fun, team-based experience**, making *Breakout Beyond* more engaging when played with a friend.

9.2 Online Multiplayer: Competing Against Others

For players who enjoy **competitive gameplay**, *Breakout Beyond* includes **online multiplayer modes,** allowing them to challenge opponents worldwide.

Online Multiplayer Modes

1. **1v1 Duel Mode**

   - Players **compete head-to-head**, trying to break blocks faster than their opponent.
   - Special blocks can **send obstacles** to the opponent's screen.

2. **Survival Battle**

   - A **battle royale-style mode** where multiple players **compete to last the longest** without losing all their lives.
   - Randomized power-ups and hazards add **extra challenges**.

3. **Team-Based Challenges**

   - Players form **teams of two or more** to **clear levels together**.
   - The fastest team to **destroy all blocks** wins.

4. **Ranked Leaderboard Matches**

   - Competitive matchmaking places players into **ranked tiers** based on performance.
   - Winning matches increases **rank and rewards**.

Tips for Winning Online Matches

1. **Master Fast Reactions**

   - Online opponents are **unpredictable**, so quick reflexes are essential.
   - Stay alert for **power-ups that change ball speed or direction**.

2. **Use Disruptive Tactics**

    ○ Some game modes allow you to **send obstacles or speed up your opponent's ball**.
    ○ Focus on breaking blocks strategically to **control the pace of the match**.

3. **Study Opponents' Playstyles**

    ○ Some players **prioritize power-ups**, while others focus on **combo-building**.
    ○ Adapting to their style can give you the edge.

4. **Climb the Ranks for Rewards**

    ○ Winning ranked matches **earns exclusive skins and leaderboard bonuses**.
    ○ Weekly tournaments may offer **special prizes for top competitors**.

Online multiplayer in *Breakout Beyond* provides **endless competitive opportunities**, making each match a unique and exciting experience!

9.3 Leaderboards and Ranking System

For competitive players, *Breakout Beyond* features a **global leaderboard and ranking system**, allowing them to track their progress and compare scores with players worldwide.

Types of Leaderboards

1. **Global Leaderboard**

- Displays the **top players worldwide** based on high scores.
- Updated **daily, weekly, and monthly** for fresh competition.

2. **Friends Leaderboard**

- Allows players to **compare scores with friends**.
- Encourages friendly competition within small groups.

3. **Mode-Specific Leaderboards**

- Separate leaderboards for **Classic Mode, Endless Mode, and Multiplayer Battles**.
- Players can specialize in specific game types.

4. **Event-Based Leaderboards**

- Special **seasonal or limited-time challenges** with exclusive rewards.
- Players compete for **rare skins, titles, and bonus power-ups**.

Ranking System in Online Play

Multiplayer matches feature a **ranked system**, where players earn **points and tiers** based on performance.

Ranking Tiers

- **Bronze** – Beginner level, learning the mechanics.
- **Silver** – Intermediate players, focusing on combos and strategy.
- **Gold** – High-skill level, competitive players.
- **Platinum** – Expert players with advanced tactics.

- **Diamond** – Top-tier, elite players competing for leaderboard dominance.
- **Legendary** – Exclusive ranking for the **top 100 players** each season.

How to Climb the Ranks

1. **Win Multiplayer Matches**

   - Victories grant **ranking points**.
   - Losing matches may result in **point deductions**.

2. **Score Big in Single-Player**

   - High scores in **Endless Mode and Challenge Mode** also contribute to leaderboard placement.

3. **Participate in Weekly Challenges**

   - Special tournaments offer **bonus ranking points**.

4. **Maintain Win Streaks**

   - Consecutive wins in ranked play **increase progression speed**.

By competing in *Breakout Beyond*'s ranking system, players can **earn prestige, unlock rewards, and prove their skills** on a global scale.

9.4 Future Updates and DLC Content

Breakout Beyond is designed to evolve over time, with **updates, expansions, and DLC content** planned to keep the gameplay fresh.

Planned Free Updates

1. **New Game Modes**

   - *Versus Mode*: Competitive battles with **special abilities and custom arenas**.
   - *Speedrun Mode*: Players race to **clear levels as fast as possible**.

2. **Additional Power-Ups**

   - *Gravity Ball*: A special ball that **warps the trajectory of all nearby objects**.
   - *Time Freeze*: Slows down the game for **precision shots**.

3. **Expanded Level Editor**

   - Players can **design and share custom levels**.
   - Community maps may be **featured in official playlists**.

DLC and Premium Expansions

1. **Retro Revival Pack** *(Paid DLC)*

   - Classic *Breakout* levels redesigned in **modern graphics**.
   - **Original sound effects and pixel-art skins** for nostalgia.

2. **Cosmic Expansion** *(Paid DLC)*

   - Space-themed levels with **anti-gravity mechanics**.
   - New alien-inspired paddle designs.

3. **Multiplayer Arenas** *(Free & Paid Content)*

   - New competitive arenas with **environmental hazards**.

- Exclusive rewards for ranked play participants.

How Players Can Stay Updated

- Developers will **post news and update logs** in-game and on official forums.
- Players can **vote on future content** through community polls.
- Limited-time events will introduce **themed challenges and exclusive unlocks**.

Chapter 10: Tips, Tricks, and Troubleshooting

10.1 Common Mistakes and How to Avoid Them

Even experienced players can make mistakes in *Breakout Beyond*, but understanding common pitfalls can help improve performance and maximize scores.

1. Poor Paddle Positioning

- **Mistake**: Staying in one spot too long or reacting too late.
- **Solution**: Keep your paddle **centered** and adjust **early** to predict ball movement.

2. Misusing Power-Ups

- **Mistake**: Grabbing every power-up without considering the situation.
- **Solution**: Prioritize power-ups that fit your playstyle. For example, don't activate a **multi-ball** when struggling to control a single ball.

3. Overreliance on Fast Movements

- **Mistake**: Moving too aggressively and missing easy rebounds.
- **Solution**: Use **smooth, controlled movements** and avoid unnecessary quick jerks.

4. Ignoring Ball Angles

- **Mistake**: Hitting the ball randomly instead of using strategic angles.
- **Solution**: Use the **edges of your paddle** to control trajectory and **target difficult blocks**.

5. Forgetting About Score Multipliers

- **Mistake**: Playing passively without maximizing combo chains.
- **Solution**: Keep the ball in play as long as possible, break multiple blocks in one shot, and aim for high-value targets first.

By avoiding these mistakes, players can improve consistency, get higher scores, and progress further in *Breakout Beyond*.

10.2 Troubleshooting Performance Issues

If *Breakout Beyond* isn't running smoothly, follow these troubleshooting steps to fix common performance issues.

1. Low FPS (Laggy or Choppy Gameplay)

- **Causes**:
  - High graphics settings on a **low-end device**.
  - Background apps consuming too many resources.
- **Solutions**:
  - Lower graphics settings (disable **shadows, motion blur, and extra visual effects**).
  - Close unnecessary apps running in the background.

- Update **graphics drivers** if playing on PC.

2. Game Crashes or Freezes

- **Causes**:
  - Outdated game version.
  - Corrupted installation files.
- **Solutions**:
  - Check for **game updates**.
  - Verify game files (Steam/Epic launcher) or **reinstall the game**.

3. Input Lag or Unresponsive Controls

- **Causes**:
  - Wireless controllers may have a **slow response time**.
  - System latency affecting input speed.
- **Solutions**:
  - Use a **wired controller** or optimize controller settings.
  - Reduce **system latency settings** in the game menu.

4. Multiplayer Connectivity Issues

- **Causes**:
  - Slow or unstable internet connection.
  - Server outages or maintenance.
- **Solutions**:
  - Switch to a **wired internet connection** for more stability.
  - Check the **game's server status** for any downtime updates.

10.3 Improving Reaction Time and Precision

Fast reflexes and precise movements are crucial for mastering *Breakout Beyond*. Here are some proven ways to enhance your reaction speed and paddle control.

1. Train Your Eye-Hand Coordination

- Focus on the **ball's trajectory** rather than just the paddle.
- Keep your eyes slightly **ahead of the ball** to predict its movement.
- Use a **high-refresh-rate monitor** if playing on PC for smoother motion.

2. Optimize Your Control Settings

- Adjust **sensitivity settings** to find a balance between speed and accuracy.
- If using a controller, test **both analog stick and D-pad** to see which offers better control.
- On a keyboard, ensure your **key bindings are comfortable** for quick movements.

3. Use Training Drills

- **Reaction Drills**: Play on faster ball speed settings to challenge reflexes.
- **Precision Drills**: Aim to **hit specific blocks** instead of just keeping the ball in play.
- **Survival Mode**: Practice **longer rallies** to improve endurance and consistency.

4. Stay Relaxed Under Pressure

- Tension slows down reaction speed—keep **a light grip on your controller or mouse**.
- Take short breaks if you notice **performance dropping due to fatigue**.

5. Learn from Replays and High-Scoring Players

- Watch **replay footage** to analyze mistakes.
- Observe leaderboard players to see **how they control ball angles and speed**.

10.4 FAQs and Developer Support

Frequently Asked Questions

Q1: What should I do if my progress is not saving?

A: Ensure you are **logged into your account** and that cloud saves are enabled. If using a console, check for **system storage issues**.

Q2: Can I play *Breakout Beyond* offline?

A: Yes, the game supports **offline single-player**. However, online multiplayer and leaderboards require an internet connection.

Q3: Why are my power-ups not activating?

A: Some power-ups require **specific conditions** to trigger. Check if you need to press an activation button or if another power-up is already in effect.

Q4: How do I report a bug or issue?

A: Use the in-game **report feature** under "Settings" or visit the **official support page** to submit a ticket.

Contacting Developer Support

- **Official Website**: [Insert developer website]
- **Support Email**: [Insert support email]
- **Community Forums & Discord**: Check the official community pages for **help from other players and dev updates**.

By using these resources, players can quickly resolve issues and **stay updated on new patches, bug fixes, and upcoming content** in *Breakout Beyond*!

www.ingramcontent.com/pod-product-compliance
Lightning Source LLC
Chambersburg PA
CBHW071030050326
40689CB00014B/3586